Our Fish & Seafood Recipes

Decorate a pillar candle with sparkly sand and tiny seashells
brought back from a trip to the beach. Simply brush
craft glue on the candle, sprinkle with sand and press in shells.
Set the candle on a saucer filled with more sand...so pretty.

Dilled Crab Egg Cups

Makes one dozen

1/2 lb. crabmeat, flaked
8-oz. pkg. cream cheese, diced
1 T. fresh dill, chopped and
　　divided
1 doz. eggs

1/2 c. milk
1/2 c. sour cream
Optional: salad greens,
　　favorite-flavor salad dressing

Divide crabmeat and cream cheese evenly among 12 greased muffin cups. Sprinkle dill into each cup. In a bowl, whisk together eggs, milk and sour cream. Divide egg mixture among muffin cups, filling each about 3/4 full. Bake at 450 degrees for 10 to 15 minutes, until puffed and golden. Cool slightly; remove from tin. Serve egg cups on a bed of salad greens drizzled with dressing, if desired.

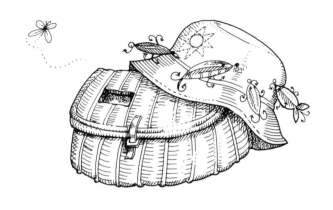

Pack up your fishing gear and head to a peaceful lake
or shady riverbank. Even if you don't catch any fish,
you'll enjoy a day of relaxing fun!

Herbed Salmon Omelets

1/4 c. sour cream
2 T. fresh dill, chopped
2 T. fresh chives, chopped
2 T. butter, divided

1/4 lb. smoked salmon, chopped
    and divided
6 eggs, beaten and divided

Mix together sour cream and herbs in a small bowl; set aside. Heat
one tablespoon butter in a skillet over low heat. Add half the salmon;
cook and stir for one minute. Add half the eggs to the skillet and cook,
lifting edges to allow uncooked egg to flow underneath. When almost set,
spoon half the sour cream mixture over half the omelet. Fold omelet over
and slide onto plate. Keep warm while making second omelet with
remaining ingredients.

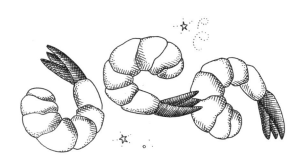

Keep frozen shrimp on hand for delicious meals anytime. Let it thaw overnight in the fridge, or for a quicker way, place the frozen shrimp in a colander and run ice-cold water over it. Don't thaw shrimp in the microwave, as it will get mushy.

Cheesy Shrimp & Grits

5 c. water
1-1/4 c. quick-cooking grits,
    uncooked
2 c. shredded Cheddar cheese
1/2 c. butter
2 eggs, beaten
1 c. milk
garlic powder and salt to taste
1 lb. uncooked medium shrimp,
    peeled and cleaned

2 t. garlic, minced
2 T. olive oil
1/2 c. white wine or chicken broth
1-1/2 t. fresh parsley, chopped
1/4 t. salt
1/2 t. pepper
1/4 c. lemon juice

Bring water to a boil in a saucepan over medium-high heat. Stir in grits; cook grits in boiling water for 5 minutes. Add cheese, butter, eggs, milk, garlic powder and salt to grits; mix well. Spoon into a greased 4-quart casserole dish. Bake, uncovered, at 350 degrees for 45 minutes, or until lightly golden. Meanwhile, in a skillet over medium heat, sauté shrimp and garlic in olive oil until cooked through, about 5 minutes. Add remaining ingredients; heat through. Top grits with shrimp mixture before serving.

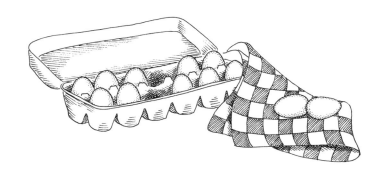

Remember that eggs will beat up fluffier for
frittatas, quiches and bakes if they're at
room temperature and not too cold.

Crab, Corn & Pepper Frittata

Serves 4 to 6

6 eggs, beaten
1/4 c. milk
1/3 c. mayonnaise
1 c. imitation crabmeat, flaked
2 T. green onion, chopped
2 T. red pepper, chopped
1/3 c. corn
salt and pepper to taste
1 c. shredded Monterey Jack
    cheese

Whisk together all ingredients except cheese. Pour into a greased 10" pie plate. Bake at 350 degrees for 15 to 20 minutes, until set. Sprinkle with cheese and bake for an additional 5 minutes, or until cheese is melted.

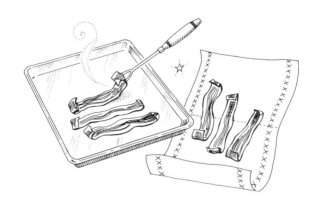

Bacon is tasty, but can be messy to fry...so bake it instead. Arrange slices on a jelly roll pan and bake at 350 degrees. It'll be crispy in about 15 minutes, plus no messy spatters!

Bacon-Wrapped Scallops

Serves 10 to 12

1/2 c. all-purpose flour
1/2 t. salt
1-1/2 t. paprika
1/2 t. white pepper
1/2 t. garlic powder
1 egg

1 c. milk
21 scallops
1 to 2 c. dry bread crumbs
7 bacon slices, cut into thirds
Garnish: cocktail sauce

Combine flour and seasonings in shallow dish. Beat egg and milk in a small bowl. Roll scallops in flour mixture. Dip scallops in egg mixture; coat with bread crumbs. Wrap each scallop with bacon and secure with a toothpick. Place scallops on a lightly greased baking sheet. Bake at 400 degrees until bacon is crisp and scallops are cooked, about 20 to 25 minutes. Serve with cocktail sauce for dipping.

How do you know when oil is hot enough for deep-frying?
Drop a bread cube into the hot oil. If it turns golden in
60 seconds, the oil is ready.

Crab Rangoon

Makes 1-1/2 dozen

8-oz. pkg. cream cheese, softened
6-oz. can crabmeat, drained
1/8 t. garlic salt

14-oz. pkg. wonton wrappers
oil for deep frying

Combine cream cheese, crabmeat and garlic salt in a bowl. Stir until blended. Separate wrappers; one at a time, lightly moisten edges with water. Place 1/2 teaspoon of cheese mixture in center of each wrapper; bring corners of wrapper together and seal well. Repeat with remaining wrappers. Heat oil to 365 degrees in a deep saucepan over medium-high heat. Deep-fry until golden and warmed through, about 3 minutes.

There's no better way to flavor foods than with fresh herbs.
Plant all your favorites for year 'round use. Some favorites are
coriander, parsley, chives, rosemary...basil, dill, garlic and thyme.

Bacon & Herb Clams

4 slices bacon, crisply cooked and
    crumbled, drippings reserved
3 T. onion, chopped
3 T. green pepper, chopped
3 T. red pepper, chopped
2 t. Worcestershire sauce
1/2 t. dried thyme

1/2 t. dried marjoram
1/2 t. pepper
1/4 t. dried oregano
1/4 t. garlic salt
1 c. butter, softened
16 clams on the half shell
1/3 c. dry bread crumbs

In a saucepan, combine one tablespoon reserved bacon drippings with onion, peppers, Worcestershire sauce and seasonings. Over medium heat, sauté until vegetables are tender; remove from heat and set aside. Using an electric mixer on medium speed, beat softened butter; stir into vegetable mixture. Spoon one tablespoon of vegetable mixture onto each clam; top with bread crumbs. Place clams on a baking sheet. Bake at 450 degrees for 10 minutes, or until golden and bubbly.

Serve Dilled Salmon Spread on slices of toasted baguette or half of an herbed bagel. Garnish with celery sticks and cherry tomatoes for an extra-special brunch or ladies' luncheon.

Dilled Salmon Spread

Makes about 3-1/2 cups

2 8-oz. pkgs. cream cheese,
      softened
3 T. lemon juice
3 T. milk

1-1/2 t. dill weed
2 6-oz. cans pink salmon,
      drained
1/4 c. green onion, thinly sliced

Blend cream cheese with lemon juice, milk and dill. Stir in salmon and green onion. Cover and chill for several hours to let flavors blend.

Keep a jar of minced garlic on hand for speedy suppers. One-half teaspoon equals a clove of garlic.

Shrimp & Bacon Bites

Makes 16 to 20 bites

1 c. cooked large shrimp
1/2 clove garlic, thinly sliced

1/2 c. chili sauce
8 to 10 slices bacon, halved

In a bowl, combine shrimp and garlic; stir chili sauce into shrimp mixture. Cover and refrigerate for several hours, stirring occasionally. Wrap each shrimp in a bacon slice; secure with a toothpick. Place on an ungreased baking sheet. Broil 3 to 4 inches from heat source for 3 to 5 minutes, until bacon is crisp.

Create a summer nook full of memories. Dress up a tabletop with seashells the kids collected at the beach and family photos that captured all the fun!

Creamy Seafood Dip

Makes 6 to 7 cups

2 10-3/4 cans cream of celery
    soup
2 c. sharp pasteurized process
    cheese spread, grated
8-oz. pkg. imitation crabmeat,
    flaked
1/2 c. cooked lobster, diced

1/2 c. cooked shrimp, chopped
1/8 t. paprika
1/8 t. nutmeg
1/8 t. cayenne pepper
1 loaf crusty bread, cut into
    1-inch cubes

In a slow cooker, combine all ingredients except bread; stir well. Cover
and cook on low setting for 2 hours, or until cheese is melted. Serve with
bread cubes for dipping.

Mushrooms are tasty! Add them to your salad only at
the last minute because they can release moisture. Dressings
may also discolor a mushroom which might look unappetizing.
Store mushrooms in a brown paper bag (never plastic)
until ready to use.

Crab-Stuffed Mushrooms

15 mushrooms
7-oz. can crabmeat, drained
   and flaked
1 slice bread, torn
1 egg, beaten

1/3 c. onion, chopped
1/2 t. seafood seasoning
salt and pepper to taste
4 to 5 T. grated Parmesan cheese
2 T. butter, melted

Remove and chop mushroom stems, setting aside mushroom caps. Combine chopped stems with crabmeat, bread, egg, onion and seasonings; mix well. Spoon mixture into mushroom caps; sprinkle with cheese and set aside. Brush melted butter over a 13"x9" baking pan; arrange mushroom caps in pan. Broil for 2 to 4 minutes, until golden and heated through.

For a quick & easy gift, line a basket with a red bandanna and tuck in a jar of Smoked Salmon Dip, a box of gourmet snack crackers and a small spreader...they'll love it!

Diggin' for Clams Dip

Makes 1-1/2 cups

8-oz. pkg. cream cheese,
  softened
1/4 c. sour cream
3 T. lemon juice
1/2 t. Worcestershire sauce
1 shallot, minced

2 green onions, finely chopped
1 T. fresh parsley, chopped
6-1/2 oz. can minced clams,
  drained
bagel chips or sesame snack
  crackers

In a bowl, blend cream cheese, sour cream, lemon juice and
Worcestershire sauce. Mix in shallot, onions and parsley; stir in clams.
Cover and chill for at least 2 hours. Serve chilled with bagel chips or
sesame crackers.

Dear Joann,
Loved the
trip! Same
time next
year!
Love
Vickie

Joann Martin
600 London Rd
Delaware, O.
43015

Our Vacation

8

Let the kids choose their own picture postcards on
family trips...punch 2 holes on the side and tie with ribbon to
make a little book. Have them sign and date the cards,
then add their comments about each site...fun mementos!

Stuffing & Seafood Bites

Makes about 2 dozen

8-oz. can minced clams
1-1/2 c. herb-flavored
    stuffing mix

1 t. lemon juice
1/2 lb. bacon, slices halved

Combine clams with juice, stuffing and lemon juice in a bowl. Shape one teaspoonful mixture into a ball. Wrap one slice bacon around each ball; secure with a toothpick. Place on an ungreased baking sheet; repeat with remaining mixture. Bake at 350 degrees until bacon is crisp, about 20 to 25 minutes.

Create quick chip & dip sets in no time. Spoon dips into pottery soup bowls and set each bowl on a dinner plate. Surround with crackers, veggies, pretzels, chips or bread for dipping.

Holiday Shrimp Butter

2 5-oz. cans tiny shrimp, drained
   and rinsed
1/4 c. mayonnaise-type salad
   dressing or mayonnaise
1 T. onion, minced

3/4 c. butter, softened
8-oz. pkg. cream cheese, softened
1 T. lemon juice
round buttery crackers or toasted
   baguette slices

Combine all ingredients except crackers or baguette slices in a bowl; beat
with an electric mixer on low speed until fluffy. Serve with crackers or
baguette slices.

Cook once, eat twice! Make a double batch of Warm Crab Puffs, then freeze half. How wonderful to simply pull an appetizer from the freezer, reheat and serve on a busy night or for pop-up get-together.

Warm Crab Puffs

6-oz. can crabmeat, drained
    and flaked
1/2 c. butter, softened

5-oz. jar sharp pasteurized
    process cheese spread
6 English muffins, split

In a bowl, mix crabmeat, butter and cheese well. Spread on split English muffins. Cut muffins into quarters; place on ungreased baking sheets and freeze overnight. Remove and place puffs in a plastic freezer bag to store. To cook, place frozen puffs on ungreased baking sheets; bake at 400 degrees for 5 to 10 minutes, until puffy and golden. Puffs may be stored in the freezer for several months before baking.

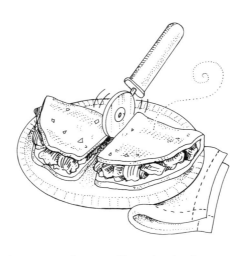

Make your pizza cutter do double duty...
it's oh-so handy for slicing cheesy quesadillas
into wedges too.

Baja Shrimp Quesadillas

2-1/2 lbs. cooked shrimp
3 c. shredded Cheddar cheese
1/2 c. mayonnaise
3/4 c. salsa

1/4 t. ground cumin
1/4 t. cayenne pepper
1/4 t. pepper
12 6-inch flour tortillas

Chop shrimp, discarding tails. Mix shrimp, cheese, mayonnaise, salsa, cumin and peppers; spread one to 2 tablespoons on one tortilla. Place another tortilla on top; put on a greased baking sheet. Repeat with remaining tortillas. Bake at 350 degrees for 15 minutes; cut into triangles before serving.

Fruit kabobs are yummy with seafood dishes.
Spear berries, pineapple chunks, melon balls or
strawberries on wooden skewers...so simple.

Smoked Salmon Canapés

Makes 5 to 6 dozen

1 c. sour cream
1/4 t. lemon zest
1 loaf party-size light rye bread,
    crusts removed
1/4 c. butter, melted

1/2 lb. smoked salmon, sliced and
    cut into 1/4-inch strips
Garnish: 2 green onions,
    thinly sliced

In a bowl, combine sour cream and lemon zest; chill for 2 hours. Brush
bread slices with butter and cut each slice in half diagonally. Arrange
bread triangles on baking sheets and bake at 350 degrees for about
10 minutes, or until lightly toasted. Let cool completely. Evenly spoon
chilled sour cream mixture onto each toast. Place a salmon strip on top
and sprinkle with green onions.

Seashells gathered on a vacation at the beach always bring back fond memories. Show them off in a sand pail découpaged with postcards from the same vacation spot.

Smoked Salmon Dip

Makes 10 to 12 servings

8-oz. container cream cheese,
    softened
2 T. fresh dill, chopped
1 T. lemon juice

4-oz. pkg. smoked salmon,
    chopped and divided
Optional: fresh dill sprigs
assorted crackers

Combine cream cheese, dill and juice in a food processor. Add half of salmon; process until smooth. Fold in remaining salmon. Garnish with dill sprigs, if desired. Serve with crackers.

New plastic pails make whimsical picnic servers for
chips and snacks. After lunch, the kids can use them
for treasure hunting around the beach.

Cucumber & Salmon Slices

Makes about 4 dozen

3-oz. pkg. smoked salmon, flaked
1 t. lemon juice
1 t. fresh dill, chopped
1/2 c. sour cream

4 to 5 cucumbers
Garnish: fresh dill or parsley
   sprigs

In a bowl, blend together salmon, lemon juice and dill. Cover and chill one hour. Meanwhile, make a design on whole cucumbers by slicing several thin strips of peel from the length of the cucumber, or scoring the peel with the tines of a fork. Cut into 1/2-inch slices. Spread cucumber slices with chilled salmon mixture; garnish each with a fresh dill or parsley sprig.

To get rid of an onion smell after slicing, simply hold your hands under cold running water along with a stainless steel spoon or other utensil.

Seaside Crab Dip

2 8-oz. pkgs. cream cheese, cubed
3 T. butter
1 bunch green onions, chopped
1 lb. crabmeat, flaked
onion and garlic salt to taste
garlic Melba toast

In a microwave-safe bowl, mix together all ingredients except Melba toast. Microwave on high setting until warm. Spoon into a slow cooker; cover and keep warm on low setting. Serve with Melba toast.

If a bunch of fresh herbs is starting to droop, just snip the stems and place the bunch in a glass of cold water; loosely cover leaves with a plastic bag, and chill. It will perk up in no time.

Shrimp-Stuffed Tomato Poppers

Makes about 16 servings

2 pts. cherry tomatoes
1/2 lb. cooked shrimp, peeled
   and finely chopped
8-oz. pkg. cream cheese, softened
1/4 c. mayonnaise

1/4 c. grated Parmesan cheese
2 t. prepared horseradish
1 t. lemon juice
salt and pepper to taste
Garnish: chopped fresh parsley

Cut a thin slice off the top of each tomato; scoop out and discard pulp.
Place tomatoes upside-down on a paper towel; let drain for 30 minutes.
Combine remaining ingredients except parsley; blend until smooth. Spoon
into tomatoes; sprinkle with parsley.

Crunchy toppings can really add fun and flavor to soup
or chili. Some fun choices...fish-shaped crackers, bacon bits,
French fried onions, sunflower seeds and toasted nuts.

Creamy Potato-Clam Bisque

Serves 6 to 8

1 onion, chopped
1 c. celery, chopped
4 slices bacon, crisply cooked
    and crumbled
1/4 c. butter
1/8 c. fresh parsley, chopped
1/2 t. salt

1/4 t. pepper
4 potatoes, diced
1 qt. chicken broth
3 T. cornstarch
1/4 c. water
1 qt. half-and-half
3 6-oz. cans clams

In a skillet over medium heat, sauté onion, celery and bacon in butter for
10 minutes; add parsley, salt, pepper, potatoes and broth. Cover and cook
for 30 minutes. Whisk cornstarch and water together; add half-and-half
and clams. Pour into broth; simmer until heated through without boiling.

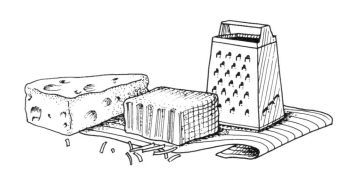

To grate or shred a block of cheese easily, place
the wrapped cheese in the freezer for 10 to 20 minutes...
it will just glide across the grater!

Pepper Jack-Crab Bisque

Serves 6 to 8

2 T. butter
2 stalks celery, finely chopped
1 onion, finely chopped
2 10-3/4 oz. cans tomato bisque
or tomato soup
2-1/2 c. whipping cream or
half-and-half

3 8-oz. pkgs. imitation crabmeat,
flaked
1-1/2 c. shredded Pepper Jack
cheese

Melt butter in a stockpot over medium heat. Add celery and onion; cook until softened. Add bisque or soup, cream or half-and-half and crabmeat. Simmer over low heat until heated through; stir in cheese. If too thick, add a little more cream or half-and-half as desired.

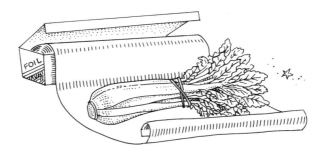

Keep celery crisp and green to the last stalk. Simply remove it from the plastic bag when you get home and keep the celery wrapped in aluminum foil.

Mom's Manhattan Clam Chowder

Makes 4 servings

3 slices bacon, cut into
    1/2-inch pieces
1/2 c. onion, chopped
1/2 c. celery, chopped
1 c. potatoes, diced
1 carrot, peeled and shredded

1-1/2 c. water
1 t. salt
8-oz. can minced clams
1/4 t. dried thyme
8-oz. can tomato sauce

Cook bacon in a heavy 3-quart kettle or saucepan over medium heat until crisp. Add onion and celery to bacon and drippings; sauté until onion is tender. Add potatoes, carrot, water and salt. Cover and simmer 20 minutes. Add clams with juice, thyme and tomato sauce. Bring to a simmer just long enough to heat through.

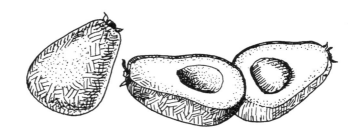

Speed up the ripening of an avocado by placing it in
a jar and completely covering with flour. Check it in a
couple of days and if the skin gives a little and
the avocado seems soft, it's just right.

Garden-Fresh Gazpacho with Shrimp

Serves 6

3 stalks celery, chopped
2 tomatoes, peeled
2 cloves garlic, chopped
1 red onion, chopped
1 cucumber, peeled, seeds removed and chopped
1 green pepper, chopped

1 avocado, pitted, peeled and cubed
1 carrot, peeled and chopped
24-oz. can cocktail vegetable juice
24-oz. can tomato juice
36 cooked shrimp, peeled

Place vegetables in a food processor; process until finely chopped. Combine vegetable mixture and juices in a large bowl. Cover and refrigerate at least 2 hours before serving. Ladle soup into bowls; top each serving with 6 shrimp. Serves 6.

A soup supper is warm and comforting on a chilly night...
it's so easy to prepare too. Just add a basket of muffins
and a crock of sweet butter. Dinner is served!

Oyster Stew

Makes 2 to 4 servings

2 T. butter
1/2 c. onion, chopped
2 8-oz. cans whole oysters,
    drained
1 T. all-purpose flour
2 c. milk

1/2 t. Worcestershire sauce
1/2 T. Cajun fish seasoning
1/2 t. dried parsley
salt and pepper to taste
1 to 2 slices American cheese,
    chopped

Melt butter in a medium saucepan over medium heat. Sauté onion in
butter until translucent. Stir in oysters; when warm, stir in flour to coat.
Stir in milk and seasonings; heat until warmed through. Stir in cheese
until melted.

Soup is extra hearty served in a bread bowl...so easy
to do for one or two! Cut the tops off round crusty loaves
and scoop out the soft bread inside. Brush with olive oil and
bake at 350 degreees for a few minutes, until toasty.
Ladle in soup...dinner is served!

Hearty Shrimp Chowder

Makes 6 servings

2 c. potatoes, peeled and diced
1/2 c. onion, chopped
1 to 2 c. boiling water
1 cube chicken bouillon
2 c. cooked medium shrimp
1/4 c. margarine, melted

1/3 c. all-purpose flour
1/2 t. salt
pepper to taste
1/4 t. dried thyme
4 c. milk, heated just to boiling

In a large saucepan, combine potatoes, onion, boiling water and bouillon cube. Cook over medium-high heat until potatoes are tender, about 10 to 15 minutes; do not drain. Reduce heat to low; add shrimp. In a small bowl, blend together margarine and flour; stir into chowder and continue simmering. As chowder thickens, stir in remaining ingredients. Simmer, stirring occasionally, until heated through.

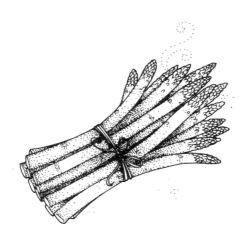

Hold the asparagus by both ends and snap off
the woody stems...they'll naturally break
right where they should!

Blue-Ribbon Crab & Asparagus Chowder

Serves 8 to 10

1/2 c. butter
1 sweet onion, chopped
2 carrots, peeled and chopped
3 stalks celery, chopped
1 t. salt
1/2 t. pepper
1/4 c. all-purpose flour
4 c. water
1/2 t. nutmeg
1 t. seafood seasoning

1 T. chicken bouillon granules
3 to 4 redskin potatoes, peeled
  and cubed
4 c. half-and-half
2 t. fresh parsley, chopped
2-1/2 to 3 c. asparagus, trimmed
  and chopped
1 lb. crabmeat, flaked
Optional: additional half-and-half

Melt butter in a large stockpot over medium heat; add onion, carrots, celery, salt and pepper. Cook until vegetables are softened, about 10 minutes. Stir in flour to coat. Slowly whisk in water; stir in nutmeg, seasoning, bouillon and potatoes. Bring to a boil; reduce heat and simmer, covered, 10 minutes or until potatoes are tender. Add half-and-half, parsley and asparagus. Simmer 10 minutes longer. Gently fold in crabmeat; heat through. Thin with more half-and-half, if desired.

Mmm...freshly baked rolls are so cozy served with
New England Lobster Stew! Tie refrigerated bread stick
dough into loose knots and arrange on a baking sheet.
Brush with beaten egg and bake as package directs.

New England Lobster Stew

1/2 gal. whole milk
2 T. whipping cream
2 T. butter, melted
3/4 t. paprika

1-1/2 lbs. cooked lobster meat
1/8 t. salt
Garnish: oyster crackers

Heat milk and cream in a double boiler; do not allow to boil. In a skillet over low heat, combine butter and paprika. Add lobster and heat slowly, gently warming the meat (do not overheat). Add lobster mixture to milk mixture and simmer on low for about 40 minutes; add salt. Serve with oyster crackers.

A tropical-themed dinner is a sure cure for chilly-weather
cabin fever. Scatter seashells and sand dollars on the
table and twine dollar-store flower leis around the
place settings...or the diners!

Thai Curry-Coconut Soup

Serves 4

1 c. onion, chopped
1 c. carrots, peeled and diced
1 c. red pepper, diced
1 c. sliced mushrooms
2 t. fresh ginger, peeled
    and grated
1/2 t. curry powder
2 T. olive oil

32-oz. container coconut-curry
    flavored chicken broth
juice of 2 limes
13-1/2 oz. can coconut milk
1/4 c. fresh cilantro, chopped,
    or to taste
1 to 1-1/2 c. cooked shrimp,
    chopped

In a Dutch oven over medium heat, cook vegetables and spices in oil for 3 to 4 minutes. Stir in broth and lime juice. Bring to a boil. Reduce heat; cover and simmer about 10 minutes, until vegetables are soft. Stir in remaining ingredients; heat through.

Need to feed a few extra guests? It's easy to stretch soup! Some quick-cooking add ins are orzo pasta, ramen noodles, instant rice or canned beans. Simmer for just a few minutes until heated through.

Bouillabaisse Gumbo

Serves 6 to 8

16-oz. can stewed tomatoes
  with jalapeños
10-3/4 oz. can tomato soup
10-3/4 oz. can chicken gumbo
  soup
3 c. water
1 c. sweet potato, peeled and
  chopped
1/4 c. celery, chopped
1/4 c. carrot, peeled and chopped
1/3 c. green onion, chopped

1 T. fresh parsley, chopped
1 T. fresh cilantro, chopped
1 T. Worcestershire sauce
1 clove garlic, minced
1 bay leaf
1/2 lb. uncooked medium shrimp,
  cleaned
8-oz. can minced clams
1/2 t. dried oregano
salt and pepper to taste

In a large pot, combine all ingredients except shrimp, clams and seasonings. Cover and simmer over medium-low heat for 30 minutes, or until vegetables are tender. Add shrimp and undrained clams; simmer 10 minutes. Stir in remaining ingredients. Remove bay leaf before serving.

To keep fish its freshest, put it into a tightly sealed
plastic zipping bag, then place into a bowl filled with ice.
Refrigerate and use within a day or two.

Fisherman's Wharf Stew

Makes 6 servings

2 T. olive oil
1 c. leek, sliced
2 cloves garlic, finely chopped
1 c. baby carrots, thinly sliced
6 roma tomatoes, quartered
    and sliced
1/2 c. green pepper, chopped
1/2 t. fennel seed
1 bay leaf
8-oz. bottle clam juice

1 c. dry white wine or water
1 lb. cod, sliced 1-inch thick
    and cubed
1/2 lb. medium shrimp, peeled
    and cleaned
1 t. sugar
1 t. dried basil
1/2 t. salt
1/4 t. hot pepper sauce
2 T. fresh parsley, chopped

Mix oil, leek and garlic in a slow cooker. Add vegetables, fennel seed, bay leaf, clam juice and wine or water; stir. Cover and cook on low setting for 8 to 9 hours, until vegetables are tender. About 20 minutes before serving, gently stir in remaining ingredients except parsley. Cover and cook on high setting for 15 to 20 minutes, until fish flakes easily with a fork. Discard bay leaf; stir in parsley.

A collection of coffee mugs is fun for serving soup!
Pick up one-of-a-kind novelty or souvenir mugs
for a song at yard sales.

Karen's Fish Chowder

Makes 4 servings

2 to 3 T. salt pork, diced
1 onion, chopped
2 potatoes, peeled and diced
1 lb. haddock, cut into chunks

12-oz. can evaporated milk
1/4 c. milk
Garnish: 1 T. butter, sliced

In a large saucepan over medium heat, cook salt pork until crisp and golden. Add onion; cook for 3 to 4 minutes. Add potatoes and enough water to cover; bring to a boil. Cook for 5 to 6 minutes; add fish and return to a boil. Reduce heat; simmer until fish is cooked through and breaks up easily with a wooden spoon. Stir in milks; top with butter. For the best flavor, make ahead of time, let cool and reheat to serve.

Create a beach scene for the party! Invite guests
to come in beach gear. Cover tables with beach towels...
put out a sand-filled kiddie wading pool and beach toys
for building sandcastles.

Simple Seafood Chowder

Serves 6

1/4 c. butter
1 stalk celery, diced
1/4 t. dried thyme
1/4 t. pepper
3 T. biscuit baking mix
15-oz. can lobster bisque
2 10-3/4 oz. cans cream of
    potato soup

3-1/2 c. milk
1-1/2 lbs. seafood like shrimp,
    scallops and crab, peeled
    or cleaned and cut into
    bite-size pieces
3 to 4 green onions, thinly sliced

Melt butter in a large heavy saucepan over low heat; sauté celery until tender. Stir in seasonings and baking mix. Add bisque, soup and milk; cook and stir until smooth. Increase heat to medium. When soup is hot, add seafood. Stir occasionally. Add green onions about 5 minutes after adding seafood. Heat until seafood is cooked through, about 10 minutes.

Keep ready-to-eat veggies like baby carrots, celery sticks,
cherry tomatoes and broccoli flowerets in the fridge...
handy for snacking anytime!

Broccoli-Crab Bisque

Serves 4

1 c. leek, sliced
1 c. sliced mushrooms
1 c. broccoli, chopped
1 clove garlic, minced
1/4 c. butter
1/4 c. all-purpose flour
1/4 t. dried thyme

1/8 t. pepper
1 bay leaf
3 c. chicken broth
1 c. half-and-half
1/2 c. shredded Swiss cheese
1 c. crabmeat, flaked

In a medium saucepan over medium heat, cook leek, mushrooms, broccoli and garlic in butter until crisp-tender. Blend in flour, thyme, pepper and bay leaf. Add chicken broth and half-and-half all at once. Cook and stir until thickened and bubbly. Add cheese; stir until melted. Add crab; heat through. Discard bay leaf before serving.

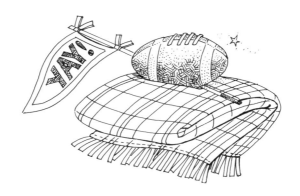

Don't have tickets to the big game? Have a tailgate party anyway! Soak up the atmosphere by going to a local high school pep rally or pre-game party. Wear the team colors and cheer them on.

Tailgate Seafood Chowder

Serves 8 to 10

1 lb. shrimp, peeled, cleaned
   and chopped
1/2 c. butter
3 8-oz. cans chopped clams,
   drained
2 10-1/2 oz. cans she-crab soup
   or cream of shrimp soup

2 19-oz. cans chunky
   clam chowder
1/2 c. vermouth or chicken broth
pepper to taste
Garnish: chopped fresh parsley

Sauté shrimp in butter in a large saucepan over medium heat. When shrimp turn pink, add remaining ingredients except parsley; heat through. Sprinkle with parsley.

A clean grill makes the tastiest foods. No wire brush handy?
Simply use balls of crumpled aluminum foil as handy
scouring pads to clean the racks of your grill.

Grilled Salmon Salad

Serves 2

10 to 12-oz. salmon fillet
1/2 c. lime juice
pepper to taste
4 c. spinach, torn
1 c. sweetened dried cranberries

1 c. crumbled blue cheese
1 c. sugared walnuts
1 tomato, sliced
vinaigrette or blue cheese
   salad dressing to taste

Dip salmon in lime juice on both sides; sprinkle with pepper. Grill over
medium-high heat for 4 to 5 minutes per side, until fish flakes easily.
Divide remaining ingredients except salad dressing among salad plates.
Slice salmon; place over salads. Drizzle with desired amount of
salad dressing.

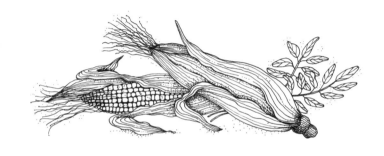

Before heating the grill, brush the rack with oil or use
non-stick vegetable spray...it keeps foods from sticking
and makes clean-up a breeze.

Grilled Corn & Shrimp Salad   *Makes 8 to 10 servings*

2 ears corn, husked
1 t. chili sauce
1/2 t. ground cumin
1/2 t. salt
1/4 t. pepper
2 lbs. uncooked large shrimp,
  peeled and cleaned
3 T. olive oil, divided
2 to 3 tomatoes, cut into
  thin wedges

1/2 cucumber, halved lengthwise
  and thinly sliced
8 c. spring mix greens
1 avocado, pitted, peeled and
  thinly sliced
Asian sesame salad dressing
  to taste
Garnish: 2 T. fresh mint,
  thinly sliced

Grill or broil corn for about 5 minutes, until lightly browned. Cool; slice
off kernels and set aside. Stir together chili sauce, cumin, salt and pepper
in a large bowl. Add shrimp; toss to coat. Heat oil in a large skillet over
high heat. Add shrimp; sauté until no longer pink, about 3 minutes.
Cool. In a bowl, combine shrimp, corn, tomatoes and cucumber; chill.
At serving time, arrange greens on a serving platter. Top with shrimp
mixture and avocado. Drizzle with dressing; sprinkle with mint.

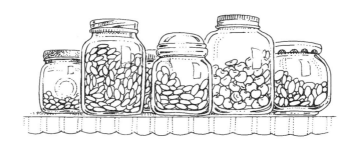

Watch for old-fashioned clear glass canisters at tag sales
and flea markets...perfect countertop storage
for macaroni, pasta and dried beans.

Italian Bean Salad with Tuna   *Makes 4 to 6 servings*

12-oz. can white albacore tuna,
    drained
2 15-oz. cans cannellini beans,
    drained and rinsed
1/3 c. capers, rinsed
3/4 c. olive oil

6 T. red wine vinegar
salt and pepper to taste
1-1/2 c. cherry tomatoes, halved
1 red onion, thinly sliced
Garnish: 1 T. fresh basil, chopped

Combine tuna, beans and capers in a large bowl; set aside. Whisk
together oil and vinegar; add salt and pepper to taste. Pour dressing over
tuna mixture; add tomatoes and onion and toss lightly. Sprinkle with
basil; serve immediately.

Serve Shrimp & Orzo Salad in zucchini boats for a summery side. Cut zucchini in half lengthwise, scoop out and place in a baking pan. Bake at 350 degrees for 10 minutes. Fill with orzo salad and enjoy!.

Shrimp & Orzo Salad

Serves 6

1-1/2 c. orzo pasta, uncooked
1 c. asparagus, trimmed
1 c. cooked medium shrimp

3 green onions, thinly sliced
1/2 c. fresh parsley, chopped
Italian salad dressing to taste

Cook orzo according to package directions; drain. Place asparagus in a large saucepan of simmering water for 3 to 4 minutes. Rinse with cold water; slice into bite-size pieces. Mix orzo, asparagus, shrimp, onions and parsley. Drizzle with salad dressing; toss to mix.

Fill the summertime picnic table with whimsies...alongside
Blue Crab Salad, serve oyster crackers and fish-shaped
crackers, watch tealights sparkle in Mason jars filled with
sea glass and serve fruit or tossed salads in new sand pails.

Blue Crab Salad

6 cloves garlic, minced
2 shallots, minced
1/4 c. oil
1/2 c. sour cream
2-oz. pkg. creamy cheese with
    garlic and fine herbs
1-1/2 t. green hot pepper sauce

1/4 t. Worcestershire sauce
1 T. fresh cilantro, chopped
2 T. fresh chives, chopped
juice of 2 limes
1 t. salt
cayenne pepper to taste
1 lb. crabmeat

In a skillet over medium heat, sauté garlic and shallots in oil just until translucent; remove from heat. In a bowl, blend sour cream and cheese; stir in sauces, cilantro and chives. Sprinkle in lime juice and cayenne pepper. Mix in garlic mixture and crabmeat, being careful not to break up the crabmeat too finely.

To clean fresh spinach easily, place the leaves
in a pan of lukewarm water. After a few minutes,
drain and discard the water, then repeat if needed.

Carolina Spinach Salad

8 c. baby spinach
2 c. seedless green grapes
1 lb. cooked medium shrimp
1 c. jicama, peeled and thinly
　　sliced

1 c. celery, thinly sliced
1/2 cucumber, thinly sliced
1/4 c. green onions, sliced
2 t. toasted sesame seed

Toss together all ingredients except sesame seed in a large bowl. Add dressing to taste. Serve on 8 individual plates. Sprinkle each serving with sesame seed.

Homemade Sesame Vinaigrette Dressing:

1/4 c. rice vinegar
2 T. olive oil
1 T. toasted sesame oil
1 T. sugar
1 t. garlic, minced

1 t. fresh ginger, peeled
　　and grated
1/2 t. salt
1/2 t. pepper

Combine all ingredients in a blender. Cover and blend well.

For a special touch when serving seafood, wrap lemon halves in cheesecloth, tie with a colorful ribbon and set one on each plate. Guests can squeeze the lemon over their dishes... the cheesecloth prevents squirting and catches seeds!

Tangy Scallops & Pasta

Serves 8

1-1/2 lbs. scallops
2 T. lemon juice
2 T. fresh parsley, chopped
    and divided
1 t. orange zest
1/2 t. salt

1/8 t. pepper
2 cloves garlic, minced
1 T. olive oil
9-oz. pkg. refrigerated fettuccine
    pasta, uncooked

In a bowl, toss together scallops, lemon juice, one tablespoon parsley, orange zest, salt, pepper and garlic; chill 5 minutes. Sauté scallop mixture in oil for 5 minutes over medium-high heat. Meanwhile, prepare pasta according to package directions. Toss scallops with pasta; garnish with remaining parsley.

Serve lemon and lime wedges with seafood casseroles...
their citrus taste is perfect paired with seafood. Guests can
squeeze on as much or as little as they'd like.

Coconut-Lime Fish Fillets

Serves 4

1 lime, halved
4 red snapper or salmon fillets
3 cloves garlic, minced
1 onion, chopped
1 stalk celery, diced

2 T. olive oil
1/2 c. canned coconut milk
1/2 c. salsa
cooked rice

Squeeze lime juice over fish fillets; set aside. In a skillet over medium heat, sauté garlic, onion and celery in oil until tender. Stir in coconut milk and salsa. Simmer for 10 minutes, stirring occasionally. Add fillets, skin-side up, gently pushing them into the sauce. Simmer for 5 to 10 minutes, until fish flakes easily with a fork. Transfer fillets to a serving platter; keep warm. Continue to cook sauce in skillet over low heat until it thickens. Ladle some sauce over fillets; serve any remaining sauce on the side with cooked rice.

Icy treats are always welcome after sizzling-hot food! For party fun, tuck wrapped ice cream sandwiches and other frozen goodies into a pail filled with crushed ice to keep them frosty.

Beachfront Crab Cakes

Makes 4 servings

1 lb. crabmeat, flaked
1 egg, beaten
8 to 10 buttery round crackers,
    crushed
1/4 c. onion, diced

1/8 t. pepper
2 to 3 sprigs fresh parsley, minced
2 to 3 T. mayonnaise
oil for frying

Combine crabmeat, egg, crackers, onion, pepper and parsley in a large bowl. Stir in mayonnaise. Moisten hands with cold water and mix well. Form into 3-inch patties. In a skillet, heat just enough oil to cover crab cakes; fry on both sides until golden. Place on paper towels to drain.

Summer humidity can cause salt & pepper to clump in the shakers. Add five or ten grains of rice to your salt shaker to keep it free-flowing. A few peppercorns will do the same for your pepper shaker and add a fresh taste too.

Pepper-Crusted Salmon

1/4 c. soy sauce
2 cloves garlic, pressed
4 t. lemon juice
2 t. sugar

4 6-oz. salmon fillets
1 T. pepper
1/4 c. olive oil

Combine soy sauce, garlic, juice and sugar in a plastic zipping bag; add salmon. Refrigerate for 10 minutes. Remove salmon from bag; discard marinade. Pat dry; press pepper into both sides of salmon. Heat oil in a large heavy skillet over medium heat; sauté salmon 2 to 3 minutes per side, or until it flakes easily. Drain on paper towels.

Large scallop shells make delightful serving containers for seafood dishes. Use shells you've found on vacation or check party supply stores for dinner-ready shells.

My Brother's Seafood Paella

Makes 4 servings

1 c. long-cooking rice, uncooked
2 c. water
1 onion, diced
14-1/2 oz. can diced tomatoes,
    drained
3 cloves garlic, minced
1 t. salt
1 t. pepper
1/8 t. saffron

Optional: 1/4 t. cayenne pepper
1/2 lb. mild fish fillets, cut into
    1-inch cubes
1/2 lb. scallops
1/2 lb. medium shrimp, peeled
    and cleaned
8-oz. pkg. frozen peas, thawed
Garnish: 1 lemon, quartered

Combine rice, water, onion, tomatoes, garlic and seasonings in a slow cooker; mix thoroughly. Cover and cook on high setting for 2 to 3 hours. Add fish, scallops, shrimp and peas; cover and cook on high for an additional hour. Serve with lemon wedges.

Change the flavor of a seafood casserole just by trying a different type of fish in the recipe. Mild-flavored fish types are cod, flounder or haddock, while stronger flavors include swordfish, tuna, salmon and mackerel.

Lakeside Fish & Veggies

Serves 4

1 lb. fish fillets
2 cloves garlic, minced
1/2 t. dill weed
1/4 t. dry mustard
1 lemon, peeled, sliced
    and seeded

2 T. butter, diced and divided
3 potatoes, peeled and thinly
    sliced
16 baby carrots
1 stalk celery, diced
1/8 t. salt

Arrange fish fillets in the center of a length of lightly greased aluminum foil. Sprinkle with garlic, dill and mustard; arrange lemon slices over top. Arrange potatoes, carrots and celery around fish. Top vegetables with remaining butter; sprinkle with salt. Fold aluminum foil around fish and vegetables, sealing well. Grill 4 to 5 inches from medium-high heat for 25 to 35 minutes.

If you're turning on the oven to bake potatoes, why not bake
a whole oven full? You can grate them and dice them for
hashbrowns, soups or casseroles, slice them for
home fries or whip up a quick potato salad!

Evelyn's Crab-Stuffed Potatoes

Serves 4

4 baking potatoes
1/2 c. butter, sliced and softened
1/4 c. light cream
salt to taste
1/8 t. pepper

4 t. onion, grated
1 c. shredded sharp Cheddar
   cheese
6-1/2 oz. can crabmeat, drained
1/2 t. paprika

Place potatoes on an ungreased baking sheet. Bake at 325 degrees for about 50 minutes, until partially tender. Remove from oven; pierce potatoes with a fork and return to oven. Bake an additional 50 minutes, until tender. Cut baked potatoes in half lengthwise. Scoop out potato pulp into a large bowl; return potato skins to baking sheet and set aside. Add butter, cream, salt, pepper, onion and cheese to potato pulp; whip until mixed. Fold in crabmeat with a fork. Spoon mixture into potato skins; sprinkle with paprika. Bake, uncovered, at 450 degrees for 15 minutes, or until heated through.

Leftover baked or grilled salmon makes a delicious light lunch!
The next day, just arrange a fillet on a bed of mixed greens
and drizzle with salad dressing.

Firecracker Grilled Salmon

Serves 4

4 4 to 6-oz. salmon fillets
1/4 c. peanut oil
2 T. soy sauce
2 T. balsamic vinegar
2 T. green onions, chopped

1-1/2 t. brown sugar, packed
1 clove garlic, minced
1/2 t. red pepper flakes
1/2 t. sesame oil
1/8 t. salt

Place salmon in a glass baking dish. Whisk together remaining ingredients and pour over salmon. Cover with plastic wrap; refrigerate for 4 to 6 hours. Remove salmon, discarding marinade. Place on an aluminum foil-lined grill that has been sprayed with non-stick vegetable spray. Grill for 10 minutes per inch of thickness, measured at thickest part, until fish flakes when tested with a fork. Turn halfway through cooking.

Try different flavors of pasta using the same recipe...there are so many to choose from! Try whole-wheat noodles or pasta flavored with spinach, garlic, basil or even spicy red peppers.

Linguine & Tomato-Clam Sauce

Serves 4 to 6

2 T. butter
1 T. garlic, minced
1 c. mushrooms, thinly sliced
14-1/2 oz. can chicken broth
2 6-1/2 oz. cans chopped clams,
    drained and 3/4 c. liquid
    reserved
14-1/2 oz. can diced tomatoes,
    drained

1 t. dried parsley
salt and pepper to taste
1/4 c. white wine or chicken broth
Optional: 1 T. all-purpose flour,
    1 T. softened butter
8-oz. pkg. linguine pasta, cooked

Melt butter in a saucepan over medium-high heat. Add garlic and sauté
30 seconds; add mushrooms and sauté one minute. Add broth, clams
and reserved liquid, tomatoes, seasonings and wine or broth; bring to a
boil and simmer for 5 minutes. If a thicker sauce is desired, whisk flour
with softened butter in a small bowl; whisk into sauce, cooking and
stirring until thickened. Serve sauce over cooked pasta.

Before cooking fresh produce, be sure to wash it well under cold water. Firm veggies and fruits like peppers and apples can be scrubbed with a veggie brush, while tender varieties like tomatoes and pears can simply be rinsed well. There's no need to use soap, but add a bit of vinegar or baking soda to the water if you like.

Basil & Tomato Halibut

Makes 4 to 6 servings

1 onion, sliced
4 cloves garlic, minced
1 T. olive oil
1 t. butter
8 roma tomatoes, diced
14-1/2 oz. can chicken broth

1 t. seafood seasoning
salt and pepper to taste
2 lbs. halibut fillets
cooked rice
chopped fresh basil to taste

In a skillet over medium heat, sauté onion and garlic in oil and butter
for 3 minutes. Stir in tomatoes, broth and seasonings. Add fish to skillet.
Cook, covered, over medium heat until fish flakes easily, about
8 minutes. Remove fish from sauce and lay on a bed of rice. Add basil
to sauce; stir and spoon over fish and rice.

Bring a little of the beach inside. Slip some
tiny seashells on lengths of copper wire, then wrap
around the stems of glasses...so pretty!

Broiled Oysters

Serves 2

1/4 c. butter
1/2 c. dry bread crumbs
1 T. grated Parmesan cheese
1 T. dry white wine or chicken
    broth

1/4 t. dried oregano
1 clove garlic, pressed
6 oysters on the half shell
paprika to taste
fresh lemon slices

Melt butter in a small saucepan over medium heat. Stir in bread crumbs, cheese, wine or broth, oregano and garlic; mix well. Spread mixture over oysters in shells. Place on a baking sheet and broil for 5 minutes. Sprinkle with paprika and garnish with lemon slices.

Stir up a delicious dill sauce. Blend 1/2 cup sour cream,
one tablespoon Dijon mustard, one tablespoon lemon juice and
2 teaspoons chopped fresh dill. Chill before drizzling
over salmon or tuna patties.

Mom's Salmon Patties

Makes 4 to 5 servings

14-3/4 oz. can salmon, drained
    and flaked
1/4 c. onion, finely chopped
1/4 c. cornmeal
1/4 c. all-purpose flour

1 egg, beaten
3 T. mayonnaise
salt and pepper to taste
2 T. oil

Combine all ingredients except oil. Mix until well blended; form into 4 to 5 patties. Heat oil in a skillet over medium heat. Add patties and cook until golden on each side, turning only once as patties are fragile. Drain on paper towels.

The next time you visit the beach, look for a piece of driftwood, empty crab shells, stones or sand dollars and make a mobile. Use nylon thread to hang them from a piece of driftwood.

Surf Side Fettuccine

Serves 4 to 6

12-oz. pkg. fettuccine pasta,
  uncooked
1/4 c. butter or margarine
1 c. tiny shrimp, cooked
1 c. imitation crabmeat, cubed

1 c. broccoli, chopped
1 c. carrots, thinly sliced
1 clove garlic, chopped
Garnish: grated Parmesan cheese

Cook pasta according to package directions. While pasta is cooking, melt butter in a skillet over medium heat. Sauté remaining ingredients except garnish in butter until broccoli and carrots are crisp-tender. Toss mixture with pasta and sprinkle with Parmesan cheese.

Watch tag sales for a big red speckled enamelware stockpot...
it's just the right size for cooking up a family-size batch of soup.
The bright color adds a homey touch to any soup supper!

Clambake In Your Kitchen

1 c. yellow onion, chopped
1/4 c. olive oil
1-1/2 lbs. new redskin potatoes
1 T. salt
1/2 T. pepper
1-1/2 lbs. Polish sausage,
    thickly sliced
2 dozen littleneck clams, scrubbed

1 lb. steamer clams, scrubbed
2 lbs. mussels, cleaned
1-1/2 lbs. large shrimp, cleaned
2 1-1/2 lb. lobsters
2 c. dry white wine or chicken
    broth
3 to 4 ears sweet corn, husked
    and halved

Sauté onion in oil in a heavy 16-quart stockpot until golden. Add remaining ingredients except corn to pot in order listed; cover tightly. Simmer over medium-high heat for 15 minutes, just until steam begins to escape; add corn. Lower heat to medium; simmer an additional 15 minutes, until lobsters are cooked, potatoes and corn are tender and shellfish open. Use a slotted spoon to arrange everything on a large platter; top with lobsters cut into serving-size pieces. Season hot broth to taste; serve in bowls.

Crisp coleslaw pairs well with fish dishes. Blend a bag of shredded coleslaw mix with 1/2 cup mayonnaise, 2 tablespoons milk, one tablespoon vinegar and 1/2 teaspoon sugar. Chill for one hour before serving.

Teresa's Potato Chip Fish

Makes 4 servings

5-oz. pkg. kettle-cooked salt &
   vinegar potato chips
4 cod fillets

4 t. mayonnaise
Garnish: tartar sauce

Measure out half the chips and set aside for another use. Place the
remaining chips in a plastic zipping bag and crush. Line a baking sheet
with aluminum foil and spray with non-stick vegetable spray. Arrange
fish on foil and pat dry. Spread mayonnaise over each fillet; cover each
completely with crushed chips. Bake at 400 degrees for 10 minutes, or
until just cooked through. Serve with tartar sauce.

Sandwiches are a tasty solution when family members will be dining at different times. Fix sandwiches ahead of time, wrap individually and refrigerate. Pop them in a toaster oven or under a broiler to eat...fresh, full of flavor and ready when you are!

Salmon BLT's

8 slices thick-cut bacon
1/2 t. sugar
4 6-oz. salmon fillets
salt and pepper to taste
1 lemon, quartered

4 multi-grain buns, split
chipotle mayonnaise to taste
8 leaves curly endive
1 to 2 tomatoes, sliced
1 c. alfalfa sprouts

Cook bacon in a skillet over medium heat for 2 minutes. Sprinkle with sugar; cook until crisp. Drain on paper towels. Sprinkle salmon on both sides with salt and pepper. Sauté in drippings in skillet over medium-high heat for about 3 minutes per side, until salmon flakes easily with a fork. Squeeze lemon juice over salmon. Spread buns with mayonnaise. On 4 bun halves, arrange 2 leaves endive, 2 slices bacon, one salmon fillet, 2 tomato slices and 1/4 cup alfalfa sprouts. Top with remaining bun halves.

Keep centerpieces whimsical. A pillar nestled in a
sand-filled bowl and surrounded by seashells
has a terrific summertime look.

Ostiones en Cazuela

1 pt. oysters, drained
2 tomatoes, chopped
1/2 c. half-and-half, divided
2 c. cracker crumbs
1/2 c. butter, melted

1/2 t. salt
1/2 t. ground cumin
1/4 t. allspice
1/8 t. cayenne pepper
Garnish: lemon or lime wedges

In a bowl, combine oysters and tomatoes; arrange in an ungreased 11"x7" baking pan. Drizzle 1/4 cup half-and-half over top. Combine crumbs, butter and seasonings; sprinkle over oyster mixture. Pour remaining half-and-half over crumb mixture. Bake, uncovered, at 375 degrees for 30 minutes. Garnish with lemon or lime wedges.

Sharing a casserole? Be sure to tie on a tag with the recipe. Clever tags can be made from almost anything...mailing or gift tags, decorative notecards, ribbons and colorful labels!

Deep Sea Delight

3 T. plus 1-1/2 t. butter, divided
1 c. onion, chopped
1-1/2 c. celery, chopped
2-1/2 c. milk
6 T. all-purpose flour
1/4 lb. Cheddar cheese, sliced
1/2 t. salt
1/2 t. pepper
1/4 lb. crabmeat, flaked
1/4 lb. lobster, flaked
1/4 lb. medium shrimp, peeled
  and cleaned
1/4 lb. scallops

Melt 3 tablespoons butter in a skillet over medium heat. Sauté onion and celery in butter until tender; set aside. Heat milk in a saucepan over medium heat. Mix in flour and remaining butter until well blended. Gradually stir cheese into mixture; add salt and pepper. In a bowl, combine onion mixture with cheese sauce mixture. Stir in seafood; transfer to a greased 11"x7" baking pan. Bake, uncovered, at 350 degrees for 25 minutes, until seafood is cooked and casserole is lightly golden.

When breaking eggs, if part of a broken eggshell
makes its way into the bowl, just dip in a clean eggshell half.
The broken bit will grab onto it like a magnet!

Delicious Tuna Quiche

Serves 4 to 6

9-inch deep-dish pie crust
6-oz. can tuna, drained
1/2 c. onion, finely chopped
1-1/2 c. shredded Swiss cheese
2 eggs, beaten

1 c. evaporated milk
1 T. lemon juice
3/4 t. garlic salt
1/4 t. salt
1/8 t. pepper

Pierce sides and bottom of pie crust with fork. Bake crust on a baking sheet at 450 degrees for 5 minutes. Spread tuna in crust; sprinkle onion and cheese over tuna. Blend eggs, milk, lemon juice and seasonings in a bowl. Pour over mixture in crust. Place pie on baking sheet; bake at 450 degrees for 15 minutes. Reduce heat to 350 degrees; bake an additional 12 to 15 minutes, until golden.

A snappy seafood sauce! Just use measurements to suit your taste. Add lemon juice, lemon zest and capers to a mixture of mayonnaise and sour cream. Sprinkle with a dash of salt & pepper.

Fresh Clam Fritters

1 c. all-purpose flour
1 t. baking powder
1 t. salt
1 t. pepper
1/2 t. cayenne pepper
2 ears sweet corn, kernels cut off

1 red pepper, diced
1 yellow pepper, diced
6-1/2 oz. can chopped clams, drained
6 egg whites
2 qts. oil for deep frying

Combine flour, baking powder and seasonings in a large bowl. Stir in corn and peppers; fold in clams and set aside. Whisk egg whites in a small bowl until stiff peaks form. Fold into batter; set aside. Heat oil to 360 degrees in a 4-quart Dutch oven. Drop batter into hot oil by tablespoonfuls; fry a few at a time for one to 2 to 3 minutes, until golden. Drain on paper towels.

INDEX

APPETIZERS

Bacon & Herb Clams, 15
Bacon-Wrapped Scallops, 11
Baja Shrimp Quesadillas, 33
Crab Rangoon, 13
Crab-Stuffed Mushrooms, 23
Creamy Seafood Dip, 21
Cucumber & Salmon Slices, 39
Diggin' for Clams Dip, 25
Dilled Salmon Spread, 17
Fresh Clam Fritters, 125
Holiday Shrimp Butter, 29
Seaside Crab Dip, 41
Shrimp & Bacon Bites, 19
Shrimp-Stuffed Tomato Poppers, 43
Smoked Salmon Canapés, 35
Smoked Salmon Dip, 37
Stuffing & Seafood Bites, 27
Warm Crab Puffs, 31

BRUNCH

Cheesy Shrimp & Grits, 7
Crab, Corn & Pepper Frittata, 9
Dilled Crab Egg Cups, 3
Herbed Salmon Omelets, 5

MAINS

Basil & Tomato Halibut, 105
Beachfront Crab Cakes, 91
Broiled Oysters, 107
Clambake In Your Kitchen, 113
Coconut-Lime Fish Fillets, 89
Deep Sea Delight, 121
Delicious Tuna Quiche, 123
Evelyn's Crab-Stuffed Potatoes, 99
Firecracker Grilled Salmon, 101
Lakeside Fish & Veggies, 97
Linguine & Tomato-Clam Sauce, 103
Mom's Salmon Patties, 109

INDEX

My Brother's Seafood Paella, 95
Ostiones en Cazuela, 119
Pepper-Crusted Salmon, 93
Salmon BLT's, 117
Surf Side Fettuccine, 111
Tangy Scallops & Pasta, 87
Teresa's Potato Chip Fish, 115

SALADS

Blue Crab Salad, 83
Carolina Spinach Salad, 85
Grilled Corn & Shrimp Salad, 77
Grilled Salmon Salad, 75
Italian Bean Salad with Tuna, 79
Shrimp & Orzo Salad, 81

SOUPS

Blue-Ribbon Crab & Asparagus
    Chowder, 57
Bouillabaisse Gumbo, 63
Broccoli-Crab Bisque, 71

Creamy Potato-Clam Bisque, 45
Fisherman's Wharf Stew, 65
Garden-Fresh Gazpacho with
    Shrimp, 51
Hearty Shrimp Chowder, 55
Karen's Fish Chowder, 67
Mom's Manhattan Clam Chowder, 49
New England Lobster Stew, 59
Oyster Stew, 53
Pepper Jack-Crab Bisque, 47
Simple Seafood Chowder, 69
Tailgate Seafood Chowder, 73
Thai Curry-Coconut Soup, 61

Our Story

Back in 1984, we were next-door neighbors raising our families in the little town of Delaware, Ohio. Two moms with small children, we were looking for a way to do what we loved and stay home with the kids too. We had always shared a love of home cooking and making memories with family & friends and so, after many a conversation over the backyard fence, **Gooseberry Patch** was born.

We put together our first catalog at our kitchen tables, enlisting the help of our loved ones wherever we could. From that very first mailing, we found an immediate connection with many of our customers and it wasn't long before we began receiving letters, photos and recipes from these new friends. In 1992, we put together our very first cookbook, compiled from hundreds of these recipes and, the rest, as they say, is history.

Hard to believe it's been over 25 years since those kitchen-table days! From that original little **Gooseberry Patch** family, we've grown to include an amazing group of creative folks who love cooking, decorating and creating as much as we do. Today, we're best known for our homestyle, family-friendly cookbooks, now recognized as national bestsellers.

One thing's for sure, we couldn't have done it without our friends all across the country. Each year, we're honored to turn thousands of your recipes into our collectible cookbooks. Our hope is that each book captures the stories and heart of all of you who have shared with us. Whether you've been with us since the beginning or are just discovering us, welcome to the **Gooseberry Patch** family!

Jo Ann & Vickie

Visit our website anytime
www.gooseberrypatch.com

1·800·854·6673